SHARK ZONE

WHALE SHARK

by Deborah Nuzzolo

Reading Consultant:
Barbara J. Fox
Reading Specialist
North Carolina State University

Content Consultant:
Jody Rake, member
Southwest Marine/Aquatic Educators' Association

CAPSTONE PRESS
a capstone imprint

Blazers is published by Capstone Press,
151 Good Counsel Drive, P.O. Box 669, Mankato, Minnesota 56002.
www.capstonepub.com

 Books published by Capstone Press are manufactured with paper
containing at least 10 percent post-consumer waste.

Library of Congress Cataloging-in-Publication Data
Nuzzolo, Deborah.
  Whale shark / by Deborah Nuzzolo.
     p. cm.—(Blazers: Shark zone)
  Includes bibliographical references and index.
  Summary: "Describes whale sharks, their physical features, and their role in the
ecosystem"—Provided by publisher.
  ISBN 978-1-4296-5414-2 (library binding)
  1. Whale shark—Juvenile literature. I. Title. II. Series.

QL638.95.R4N892 2011
597.3—dc22   2010024840

Editorial Credits
Christopher L. Harbo, editor; Juliette Peters, designer; Eric Manske, production specialist

Photo Credits
Alamy/Art Directors & TRIP, 28–29; Jeff Rotman, 19; Reinhard Dirscherl, 22–23; Stephen
      Frink Collection, 26
Ardea/B. + P. Boyle, 16
Dreamstime/Hbbolten, 9; Jamiegodson, 6
Minden Pictures/Flip Nicklin, 24–25
Peter Arnold/Doug Perrine, cover, 10–11; Jeffery L. Rotman, 12; Jonathan Bird, 21
Photolibrary/Oxford Scientific/Luis Javier Sandoval, 14–15; Pacific Stock/Watt Jim, 5

Artistic Effects
Shutterstock/artida; Eky Studio; Giuseppe_R

Printed in the United States of America in Stevens Point, Wisconsin.
092010   005934WZS11

TABLE OF CONTENTS

CHAPTER 1

A WHALE OF A SHARK

A huge whale shark glides through the sea. It whips its tail to the side and turns toward a group of small fish.

The shark opens its huge
mouth. It sucks in the fish like
a vacuum cleaner. The whale
shark just ate lunch.

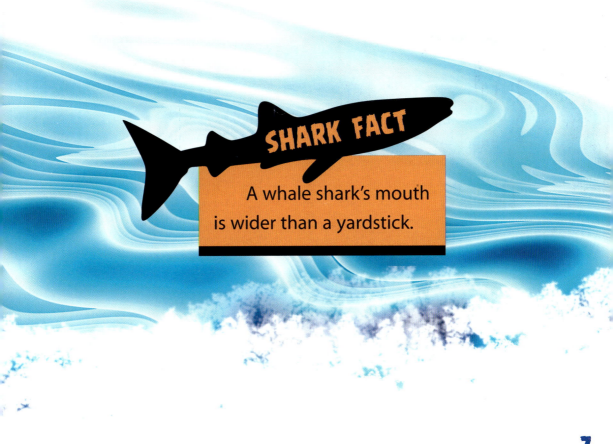

SHARK FACT

A whale shark's mouth
is wider than a yardstick.

CHAPTER 2

HUGE HUNTER

Whale sharks are the largest fish in the sea. They grow to 40 feet (12 meters) long. They weigh up to 47,000 pounds (21,320 kilograms).

size comparison

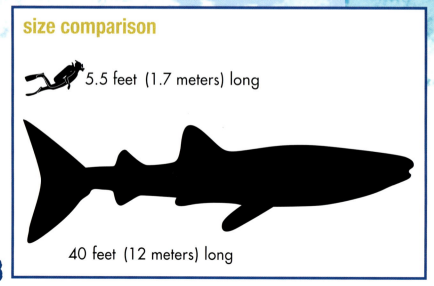

5.5 feet (1.7 meters) long

40 feet (12 meters) long

SHARK FACT

The largest whale shark measured was more than 66 feet (20 m) long. It weighed nearly 75,000 pounds (34,020 kg).

The whale shark has a checkerboard pattern on its back. Light spots and stripes crisscross the shark's dark body.

SHARK FACT

Every whale shark has different markings. Their patterns help scientists identify individual whale sharks.

Whale sharks are slow swimmers. Their large, curved tails sway from side to side as they swim. Their top speed is only about 5 miles (8 kilometers) per hour.

SHARK FACT

Sharks and whales move their tails in different ways. A shark moves its tail from side to side. A whale moves its tail up and down.

Whale sharks have wide, flat heads. The whale shark's mouth stretches 4.5 feet (1.4 m) wide. It holds 300 rows of tiny hooked teeth.

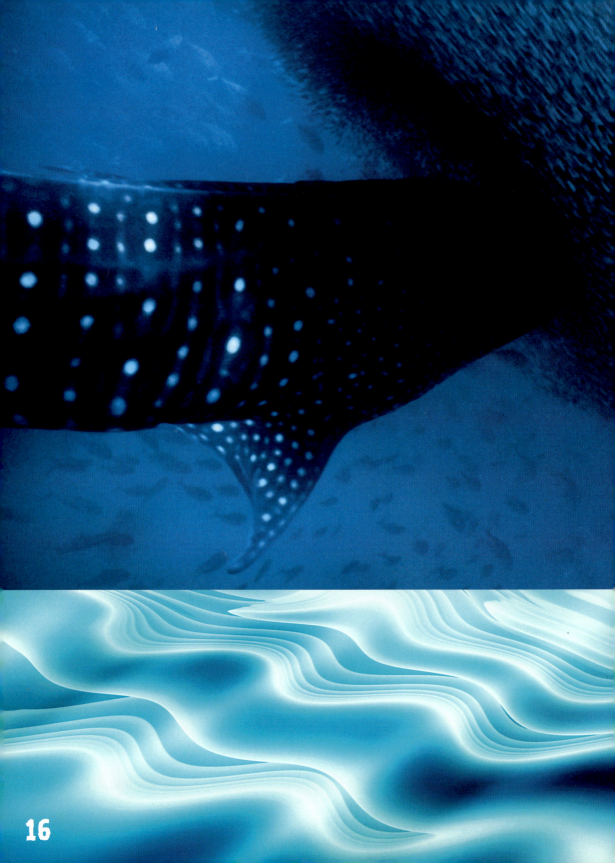

The world's largest fish eats some of the world's smallest **prey**. Whale sharks mainly eat **plankton**. They also like sardines, anchovies, mackerel, and squid.

SHARK FACT

Whale sharks use their excellent eyesight to find food. They look for patches of plankton near the ocean's surface.

prey—an animal hunted by another animal for food

plankton—tiny plants and animals that drift in the sea

gills

Whale sharks are filter feeders. They open their huge mouths to suck in prey. Water escapes through their **gills**. The gills have screens that trap the food so it stays in the mouth.

SHARK FACT

Whale sharks can filter more than 1,585 gallons (6,000 liters) of seawater in an hour.

gill—a body part that a fish uses to breathe; gills are the slits on the sides of a shark's head

CHAPTER 3

OCEAN TREKKER

Whale sharks live in all of the world's oceans. They like to swim in the warm waters of the open sea. They sometimes swim close to shore to find food.

Whale Shark Range

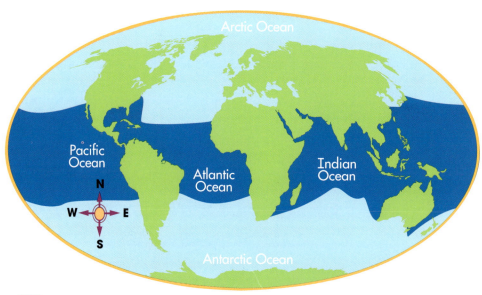

Arctic Ocean

Pacific Ocean

Atlantic Ocean

Indian Ocean

N

W E

S

Antarctic Ocean

where whale sharks live

SHARK FACT

Whale sharks usually live and travel alone.

Whale sharks don't wait for prey to come to them. They **migrate** long distances to find food. Although slow, they can swim more than 1,240 miles (2,000 km) in two months.

migrate—to move from one place to another to find food.

SHARK FACT

Whale sharks are deep divers. They can dive 2,300 feet (700 m) below the water's surface.

Whale sharks often swim with groups of large fish. Whale sharks and these fish are attracted to plankton. Fishermen follow whale sharks to catch the large fish.

CHAPTER 4

GENTLE GIANT

Whale sharks are not dangerous to people. Many people swim and dive with them. The biggest danger to divers is being struck by the shark's large tail.

SHARK FACT

People swim with whale sharks in Australia, Mexico, and Central America.

Whale shark populations are **threatened**. People hunt whale sharks for their meat, skin, and liver oil. In many countries, laws protect whale sharks from overhunting.

threatened—in danger of dying out

SHARK FACT

Hunters fire spearlike harpoons at whale sharks. The sharks are easy to spot because they often swim near the sea surface.

Glossary

anchovy (AN-choh-vee)—a small, edible fish

gill (GIL)—a body part that a fish uses to breathe; gills are the slits on the sides of a shark's head

harpoon (har-POON)—a long spear with an attached rope that can be thrown or shot out of a special gun

mackerel (MAK-uh-ruhl)—a shiny, dark blue saltwater fish that can be eaten

migrate (MYE-grate)—to move from one place to another to find food

plankton (PLANGK-tuhn)—tiny plants and animals that drift in the sea

prey (PRAY)—an animal hunted by another animal for food

sardine (sar-DEEN)—a small saltwater fish often sold in cans for food

threatened (THRET-uhnd)—in danger of dying out

Read More

Doubilet, David, and Jennifer Hayes. *Face to Face with Sharks.* Washington, D.C.: National Geographic, 2009.

Mathea, Heidi. *Whale Sharks.* Sharks. Edina, Minn.: Abdo Pub. Co., 2011.

Randolph, Joanne. *The Whale Shark: Gentle Giant.* Sharks: Hunters of the Deep. New York: The Rosen Pub. Group's PowerKids Press, 2007.

Internet Sites

FactHound offers a safe, fun way to find Internet sites related to this book. All of the sites on FactHound have been researched by our staff.

Here's all you do:

Visit *www.facthound.com*

Type in this code: 9781429654142

Super-cool stuff! Check out projects, games and lots more at **www.capstonekids.com**

Index